How To Draw FASHION

Published by Anna Nadler Art

www.annanadlerart.com

ISBN: 978-1-958428-17-7

Table of Contents

Table of Contents

Anna Nadler is a book illustrator who lives and works in New York City. She has been drawing since the age of two - it's been her life-long passion and career for several decades. Anna has taught both kids and adults how to draw, and has finally decided to put some of that knowledge into a series of comprehensive books - for everyone to benefit.

Anna has a special passion for fashion. She studied fashion design and illustration, then went on to become a graphic designer and book illustrator. You can find many of her coloring books, children's books, and more online and in stores.

Hello, fashion illustrators!

Fashion illustration is an extremely fun form of illustration that lets you express your style, unique vision, fashion flare, creativity and imagination!

Drawing fashion figures is a bit different from drawing regular figures.

In fashion illustration, our main goal is to showcase the garment, not get into the details of features or body (unless it helps to emphasize certain fashion accessories, like in a portrait wearing a hat or sunglasses.)

So, in sketching the figure, when we draw hands, we don't have to draw individual fingers, when we draw eyes, we don't have to render every eyelash, etc.

Often, a simple line is all you need to show features and the shape of the figure.

Remember, your main goal is to express the mood, beauty and flare of the garment the person is wearing.

Feel free to use color pencils to color the designs you draw in this book.

The goal of this book is to teach you to simplify, distill and learn to express yourself in as few fast lines as possible.
The more expressive your lines are, the more your illustrations will start to look stylish and unique, which works so well for fashion in particular.
Once you learn to draw quick expressive sketches, you can move on to more detailed, yet still expressive fashion illustrations.

Now let's get started on showing some differences between a regular figure and a fashion figure. Flip the page to get on your fashion illustration journey!

Sketching a Fashion figure vs. a Regular figure (female)
smaller head
fashion posture
narrower waist & hips
tall stature
longer legs
symmetry is more evident
larger head
regular posture
wider waist & hips
shorter stature
shorter legs
symmetry is not as important

Practice drawing figures of different proportions.

top of head

bottom of head

chest

waist

hips

knees

bottom of feet

top of head

bottom of head

chest

waist

hips

knees

bottom of feet

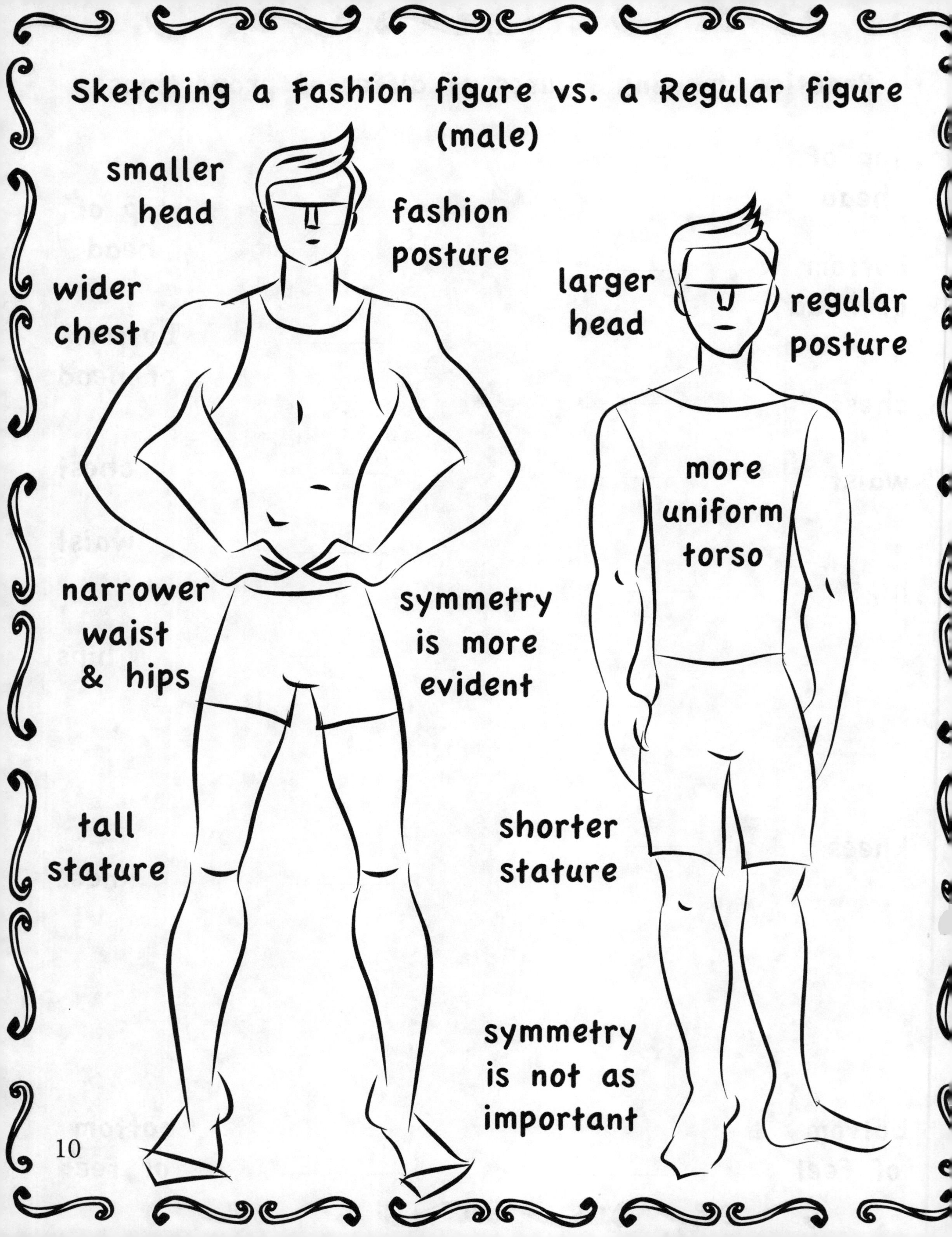
Sketching a Fashion figure vs. a Regular figure
(male)
smaller head
fashion posture
wider chest
larger head
regular posture
more uniform torso
narrower waist & hips
symmetry is more evident
tall stature
shorter stature
symmetry is not as important

Practice drawing figures of different proportions.

top of head

bottom of head

chest

waist

hips

knees

bottom of feet

top of head

bottom of head

chest

waist

hips

knees

bottom of feet

Drawing front and side view poses, women

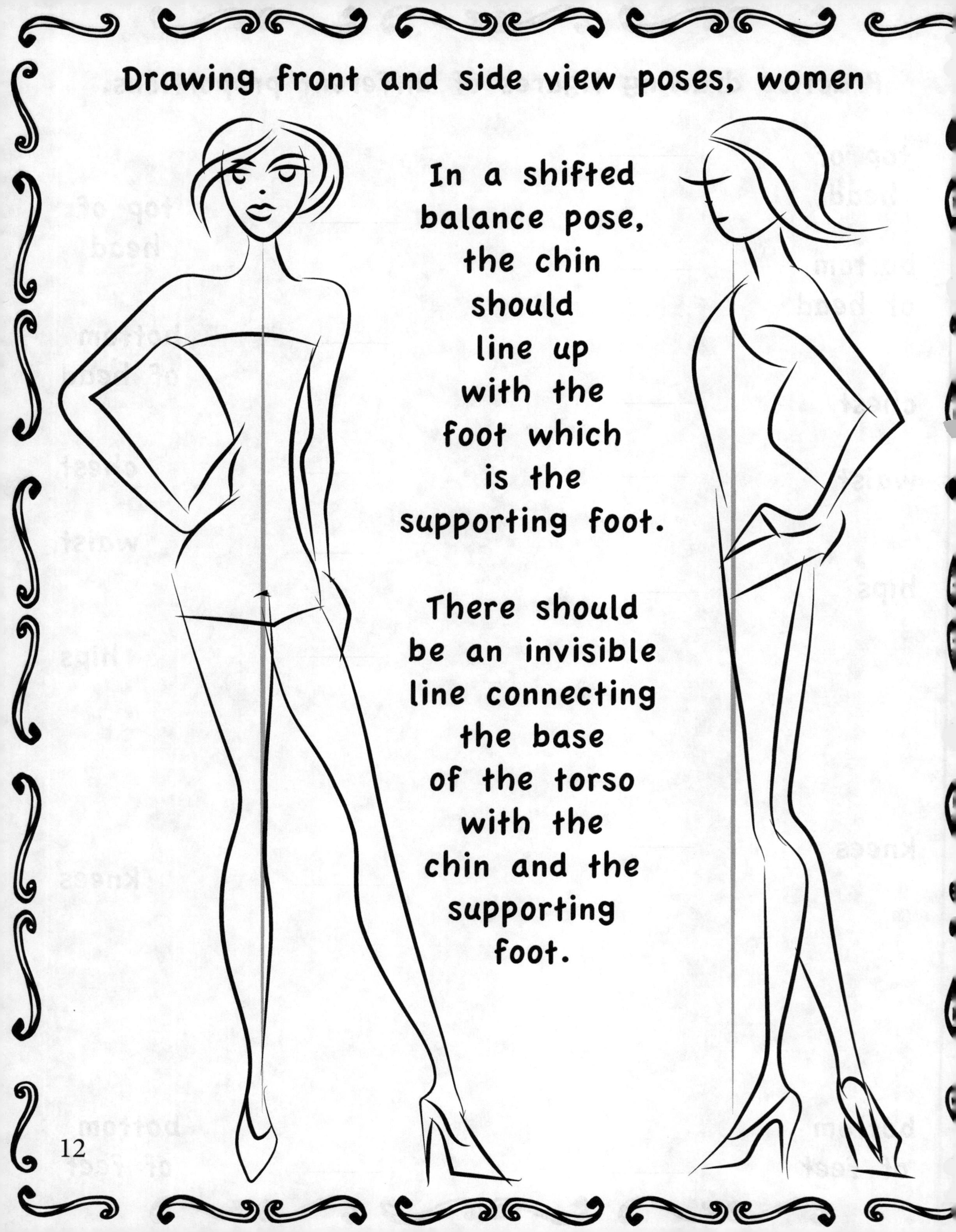

In a shifted balance pose, the chin should line up with the foot which is the supporting foot.

There should be an invisible line connecting the base of the torso with the chin and the supporting foot.

Drawing front and side view poses, practice

Front

Side

Now let us practice drawing fashion poses - front and side views.

Make sure your figure is actually "standing" firmly and does not appear falling or floating, by following the tip on the opposite page.

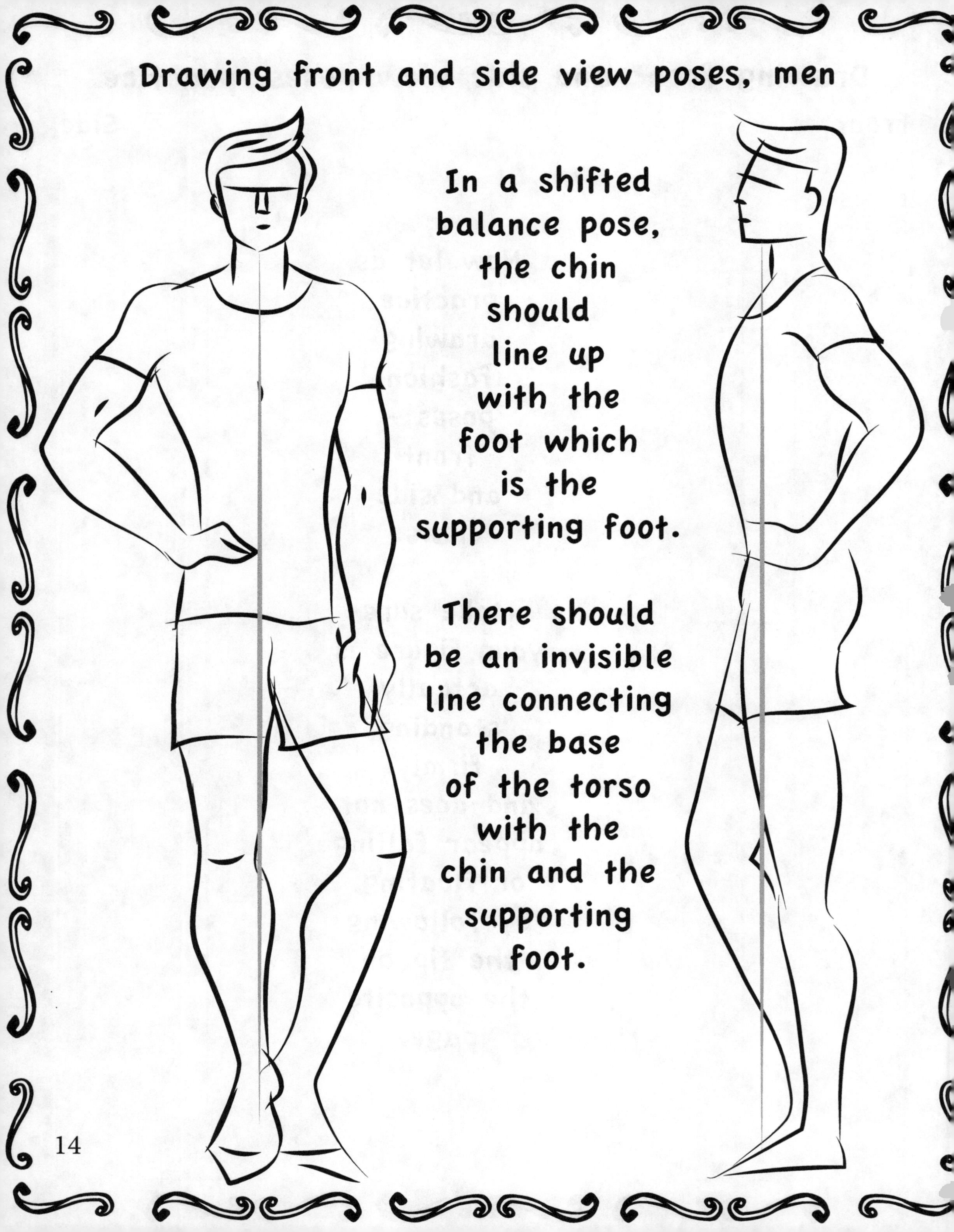
Drawing front and side view poses, men
In a shifted balance pose, the chin should line up with the foot which is the supporting foot.
There should be an invisible line connecting the base of the torso with the chin and the supporting foot.

Drawing front and side view poses, practice

Front

Side

Now let us practice drawing fashion poses - front and side views.

Make sure your figure is actually "standing" firmly and does not appear falling or floating, by following the tip on the opposite page.

Drawing female and male faces. Differences.

Female faces are more delicate, oval shaped. Women have bigger eyes and lips. Smaller nose and chin. They have a narrow, delicate neck and flowing hair with more details. Pay special attention to the way you draw women's lips, eyes and hair, especially in fashion portraits.

Male faces are more rugged, square shaped. Men have smaller eyes and lips. Larger nose and chin. They have a wide, masculine neck and simpler, messier hair. When you draw male facial features, use less detail and lines, especially when you draw things like lips and eyes.

Drawing female and male faces. Practice.

Look at the adjacent page and
try to draw the female
and male features on
the models.
Pay attention to the
differences between
facial features of
women and men.

How to draw hats

Drawing hats can be a challenge at first. Often kids and adults tend to draw hats as a separate attachment on top of the head. This is incorrect. You have to make the hats visibly enclose part of the head, with part of the head submerged inside of the hat. So you will only see about 3/4 to a half of the face. See illustration below:

Correct

Incorrect

Different kinds of hats

Hats come in different styles, shapes, sizes, designs, purposes. They can enhance an outfit, they can make someone look older or younger, fancier or more rugged. We can use hats in our fashion drawings to enhance or embellish the outfits. For our purposes in this book we will show the hats as they appear worn by people. While hats themselves are easy to illustrate, it can be more challenging to draw actual people wearing hats.

Drawing different fashion hats

Women's summer hats

Drawing different fashion hats practice. Put hats on the heads as you see on the opposite page.

Drawing different fashion hats

Women's winter hats

Drawing different winter hats

Put hats on the heads as you see on the opposite page, you can add scarves also.

Drawing different fashion hats

Men's hats

Drawing different fashion hats

Men's hats practice page - add hats!

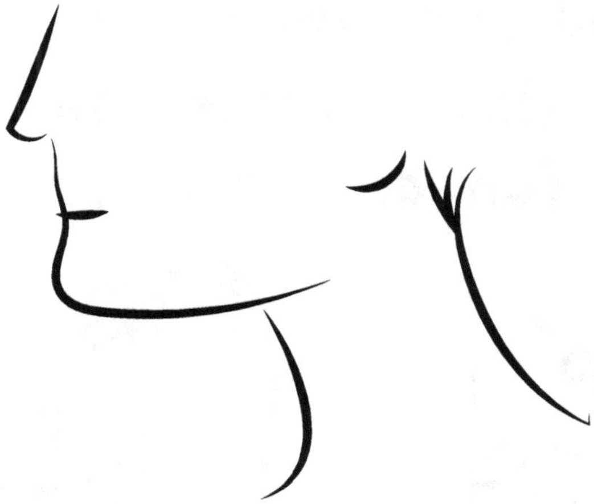

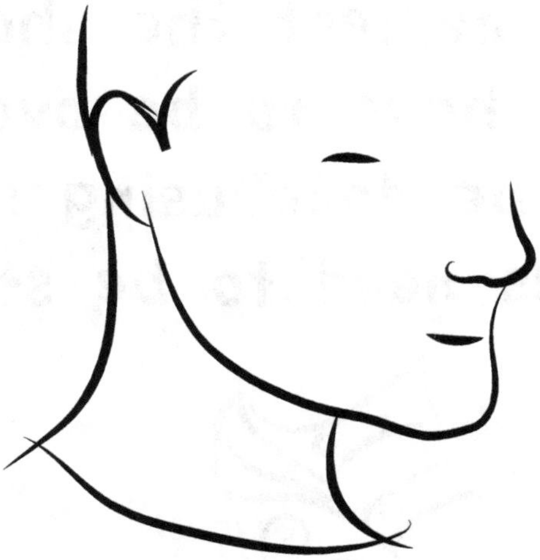

How to draw shoes

Drawing shoes is a fun way to spice up our fashion illustrations. In fact, as a creative activity, you should take one of the shoes out of your closet and spend time on studying the way a shoe is constructed, its stitching, heel, the way the material goes around the shoe, what buttons, laces, zippers, etc does the shoe have?

Fashion illustration should be anything but boring! So, the more funky we make our shoe illustrations look, the more flare and interest our drawings will have. So, when you choose to draw a full body, including feet, do not neglect the shoe. The details don't have to be over-rendered, they can be done using simple lines, but these lines need to be strong, fun and expressive!

If the shoe fits...

For our purposes in this book, we will practice drawing shoes on feet. Because it's one thing to know how to draw a shoe well, and it's another to actually show a shoe as it appears on a foot and leg.

The drawing has to be simple but believable. Practice drawing shoes you have as you see them on feet at different angles, to get the most idea of what shoes on feet look like.

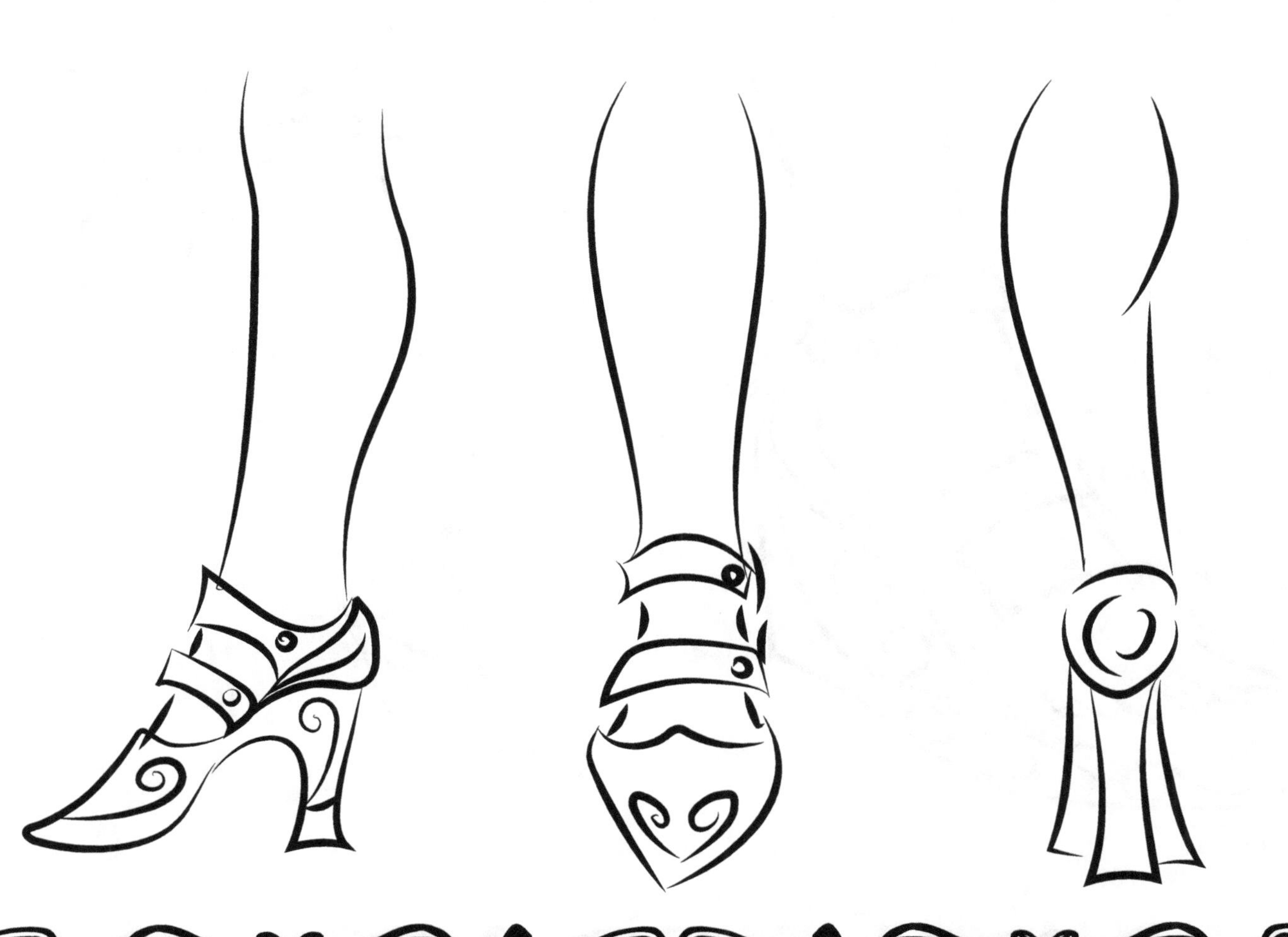

Drawing shoes on feet

Sandals

Drawing shoes on feet
Sandals practice page

Drawing shoes on feet

Dress shoes

Drawing shoes on feet

Dress shoes practice

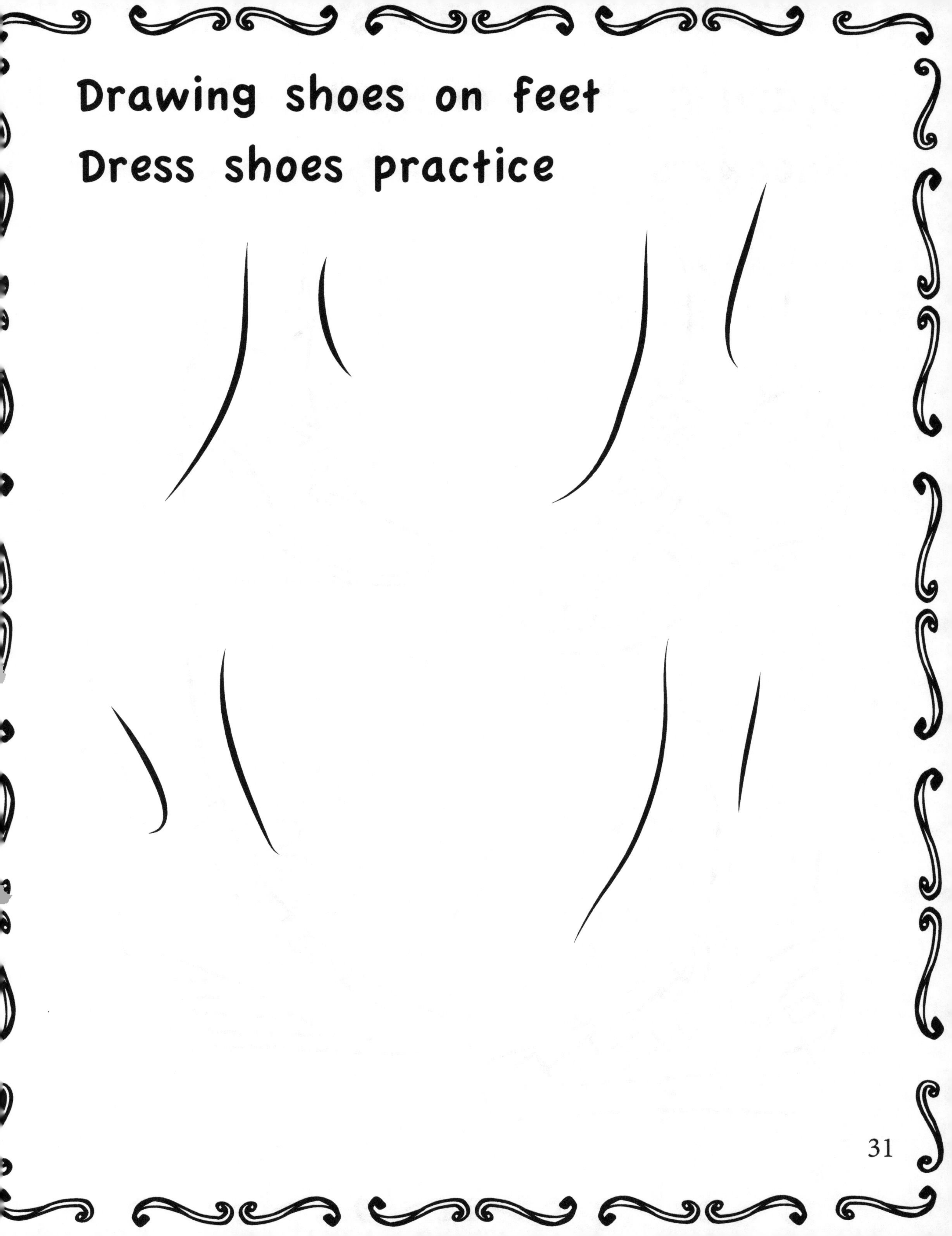

Drawing shoes on feet

Sneakers

Drawing shoes on feet

Sneaker drawing practice

Drawing shoes on feet

Men's shoes

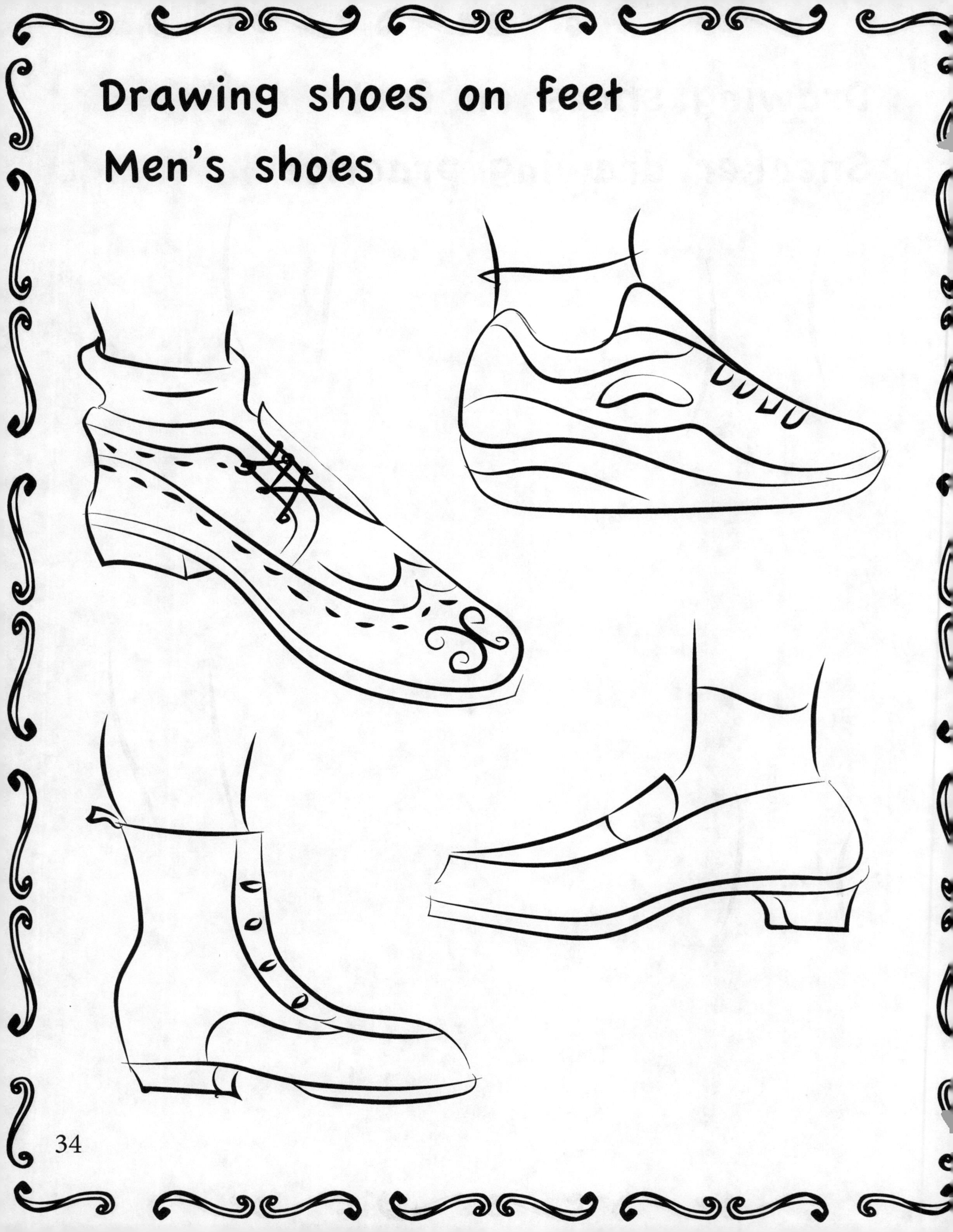

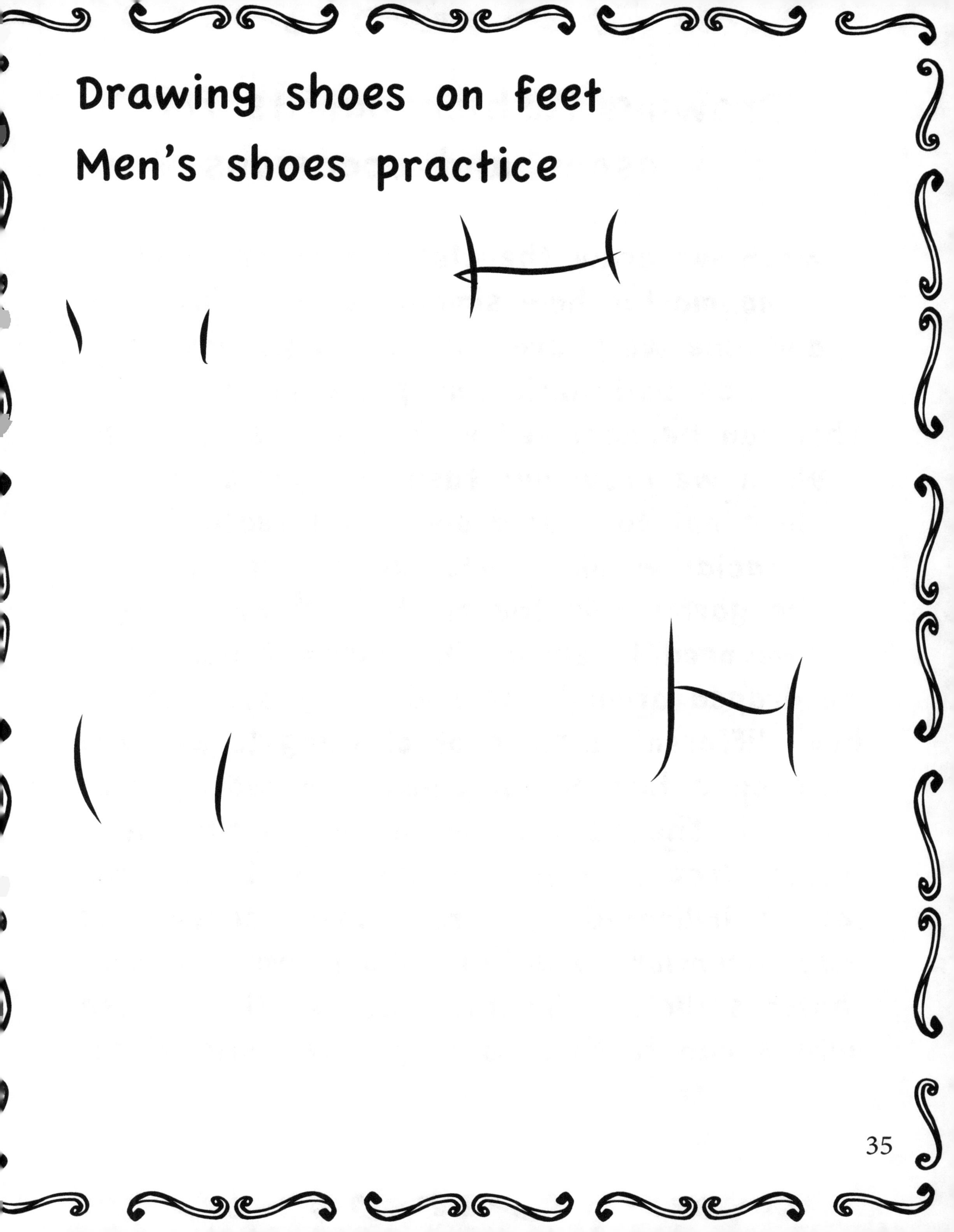

Drawing shoes on feet

Men's shoes practice

Drawing fashion outfits for seasons and occasions

When we draw the clothing on the body, no matter how simple our drawings and line work are, the drawings have to be believable and professional. This can be achieved with a few simple tips. When we draw our fashion figures, make sure not to over-draw facial features, facial wrinkles, etc. Remember that the garment is the most important thing we need to show. The garment has to be draped around the body. Pay attention to how different a piece of clothing looks when it's on a hanger vs. when it is worn by a model. The garment worn by a model has folds, drapes, it goes around the body. This can be indicated by a few simple curvy lines. Pay attention to details like prints, patterns buttons, belts, zippers, ties, as all of those details can further portray a realistic effect.

FASHION
is a very
fluid thing. Often
men can wear elements
of women's clothing and
women can be seen
in menswear.

The example fashion drawings
in this book tend to lean
towards more traditional
male and female garments,
but that does not mean
that you should not try
to experiement more in
your own fashion
illustrations.

Evening Dresses

Evening dresses are usually simple and elegant, with slick and shapely silhouettes. The models often have their hair up. They can have accessories like earrings, necklaces, bracelets, a small clutch, a boa, or a simple belt.

Evening
Dresses
- practice
Add your own
dress designs
to these figures.
Add your own
jewelry and bags.
Give them
hair styles.

Eveningwear for Men

When drawing evening wear for men, we draw elegant, clean lines. Make sure not to over-draw the face or the hair. Simple is best. Pay attention to the details of the garment. Look for references on-line for men's formal wear.

Eveningwear
for Men Practice

Fall Outfits - Women

Fall means lots
of accessories like
scarves, bags,
cute boots.
Fall means lavish
warm sweaters,
elegant lined jackets
and cardigans.
We see lots of
argyle print,
leopard print,
hounds tooth
print and more.

Indicate with
simple lines that
the garments drape
around the figure.
We want them to
be "wearing"
the clothes.
You can also show
folds and drapes
in the same
fashion.
All you really need
are a couple of very
simple small lines
and you will
portray the
impression of
clothing on the body.

Fall Outfits - practice

Now let's practice drawing fall fashion. Find references on-line for many different fall styles. You can get inspired by them and create your own versions. You can also survey your own closet for some accessories, boots, scarves, etc.

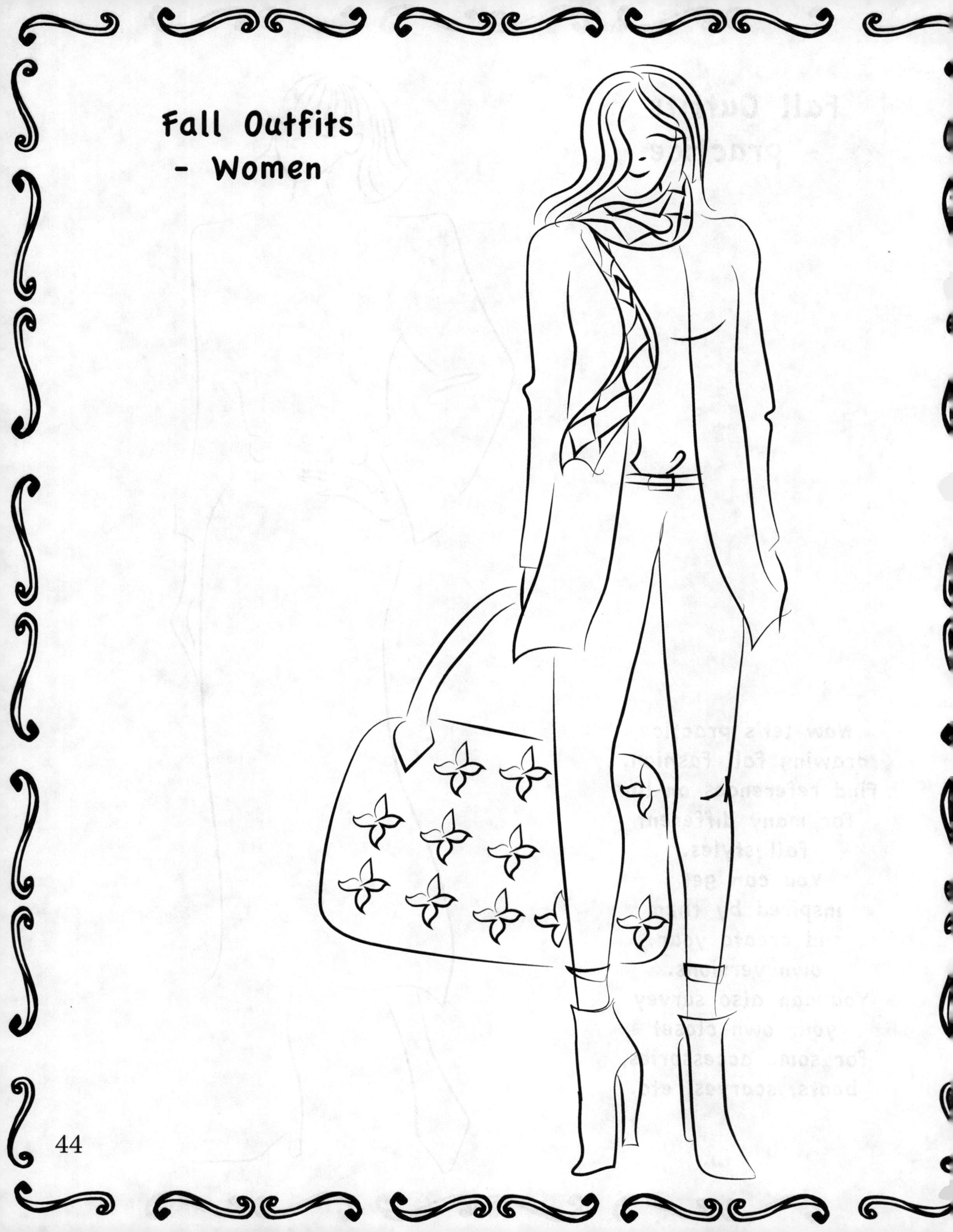

Fall Outfits - Women

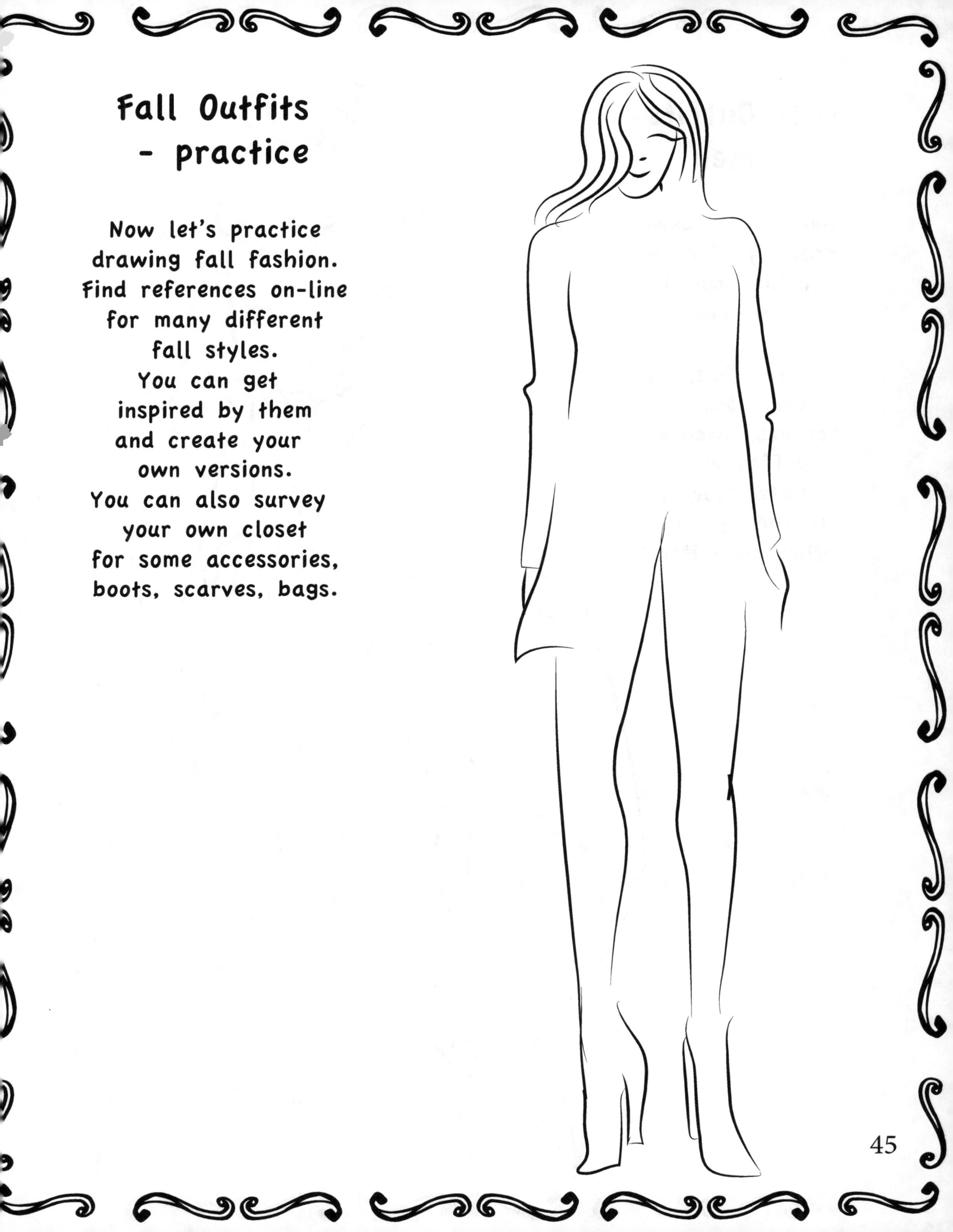

Fall Outfits - practice

Now let's practice drawing fall fashion. Find references on-line for many different fall styles. You can get inspired by them and create your own versions. You can also survey your own closet for some accessories, boots, scarves, bags.

Fall Outfits - Men

Here is a closeup drawing of a fall fashion outfit for men.

In the fall, we wear lots of scarves, sweaters, puffed vests, hats, gloves, leather jackets, other cozy items.

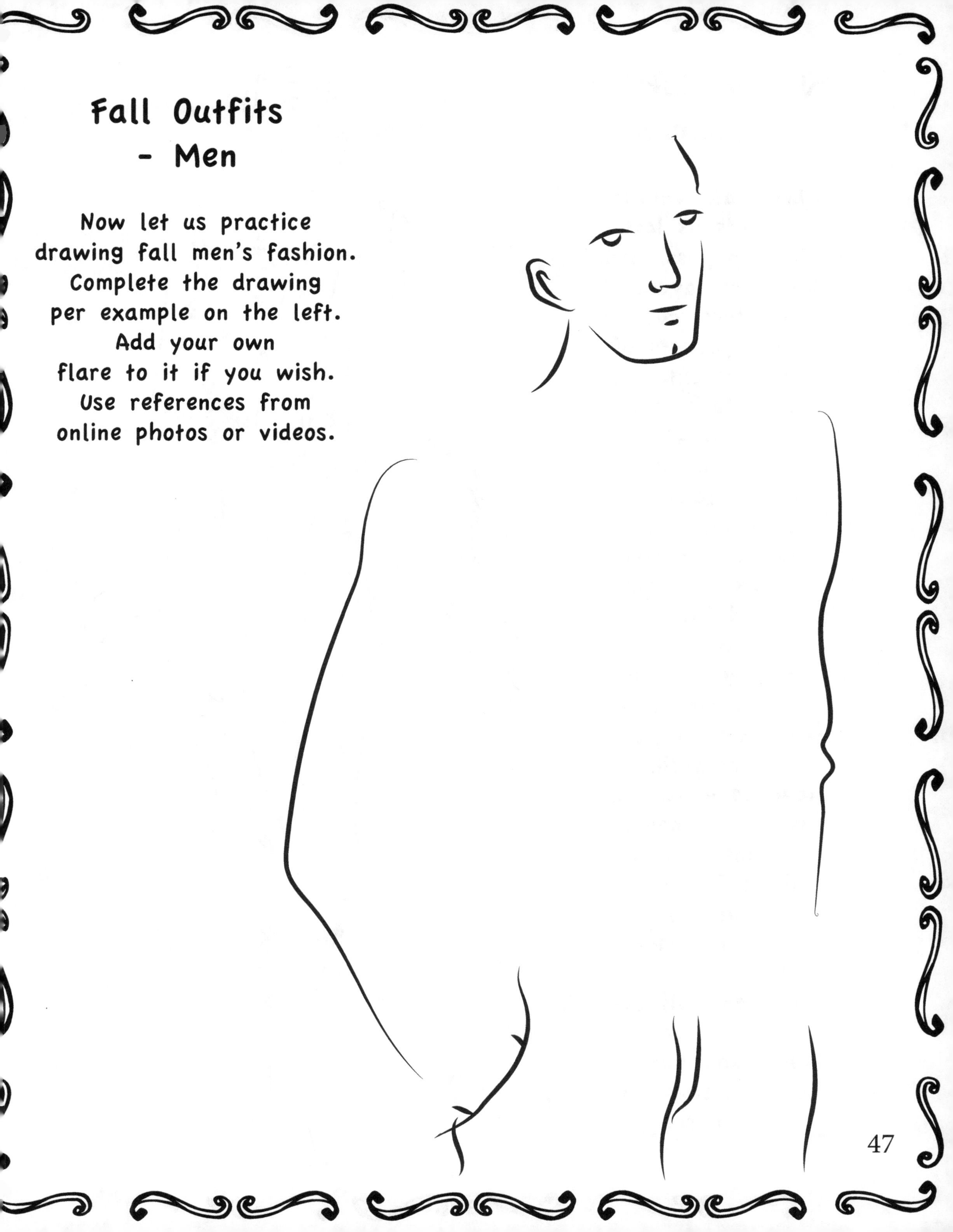

Fall Outfits - Men

Now let us practice drawing fall men's fashion. Complete the drawing per example on the left. Add your own flare to it if you wish. Use references from online photos or videos.

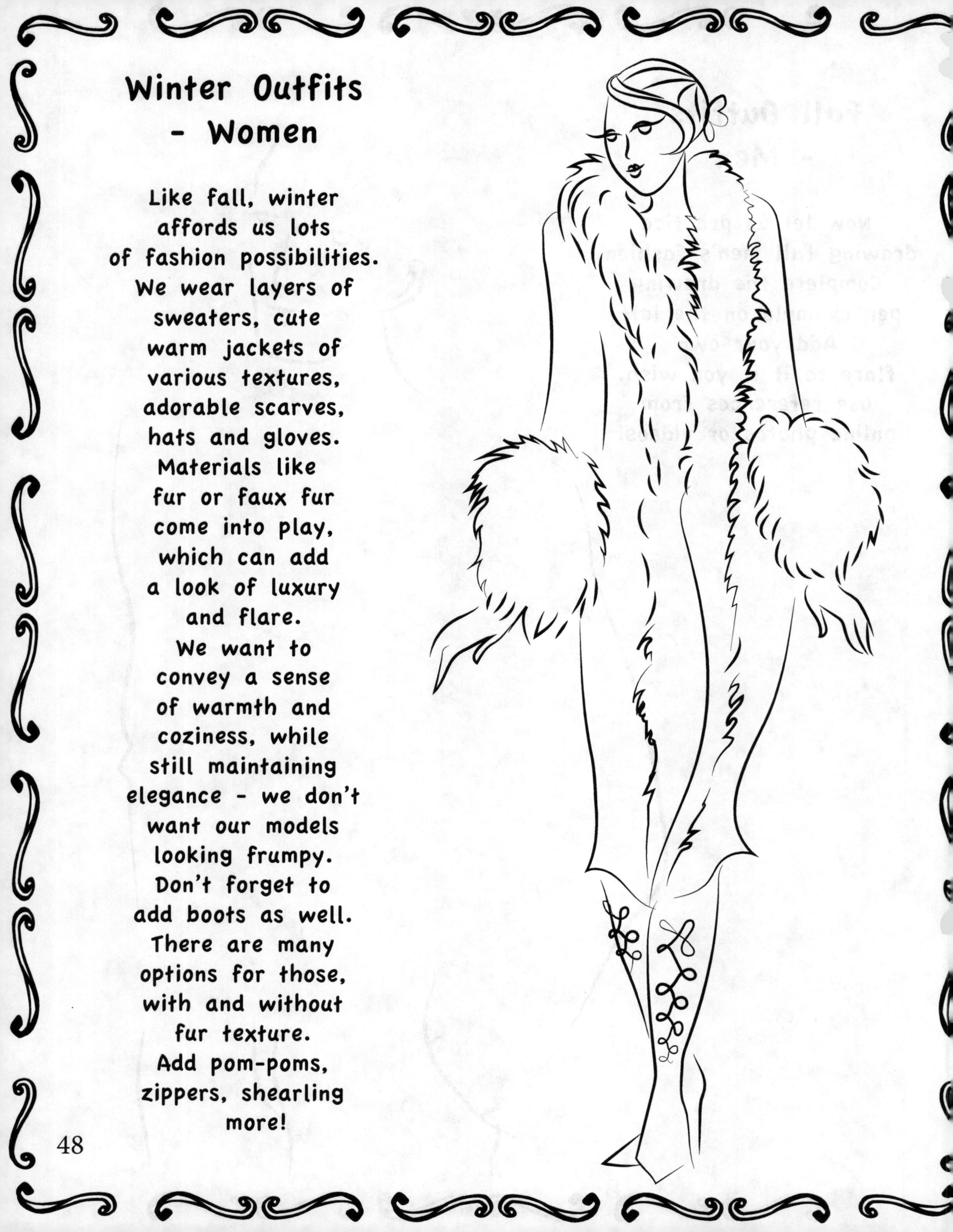

Winter Outfits - Women

Like fall, winter affords us lots of fashion possibilities. We wear layers of sweaters, cute warm jackets of various textures, adorable scarves, hats and gloves. Materials like fur or faux fur come into play, which can add a look of luxury and flare. We want to convey a sense of warmth and coziness, while still maintaining elegance - we don't want our models looking frumpy. Don't forget to add boots as well. There are many options for those, with and without fur texture. Add pom-poms, zippers, shearling more!

Winter Outfits - Practice

Now let's practice drawing winter fashion. Find references on-line for many different winter styles. You can get inspired by them and create your own versions. You can also survey your own closet for some accessories, boots, coats, scarves, gloves, bags, etc.

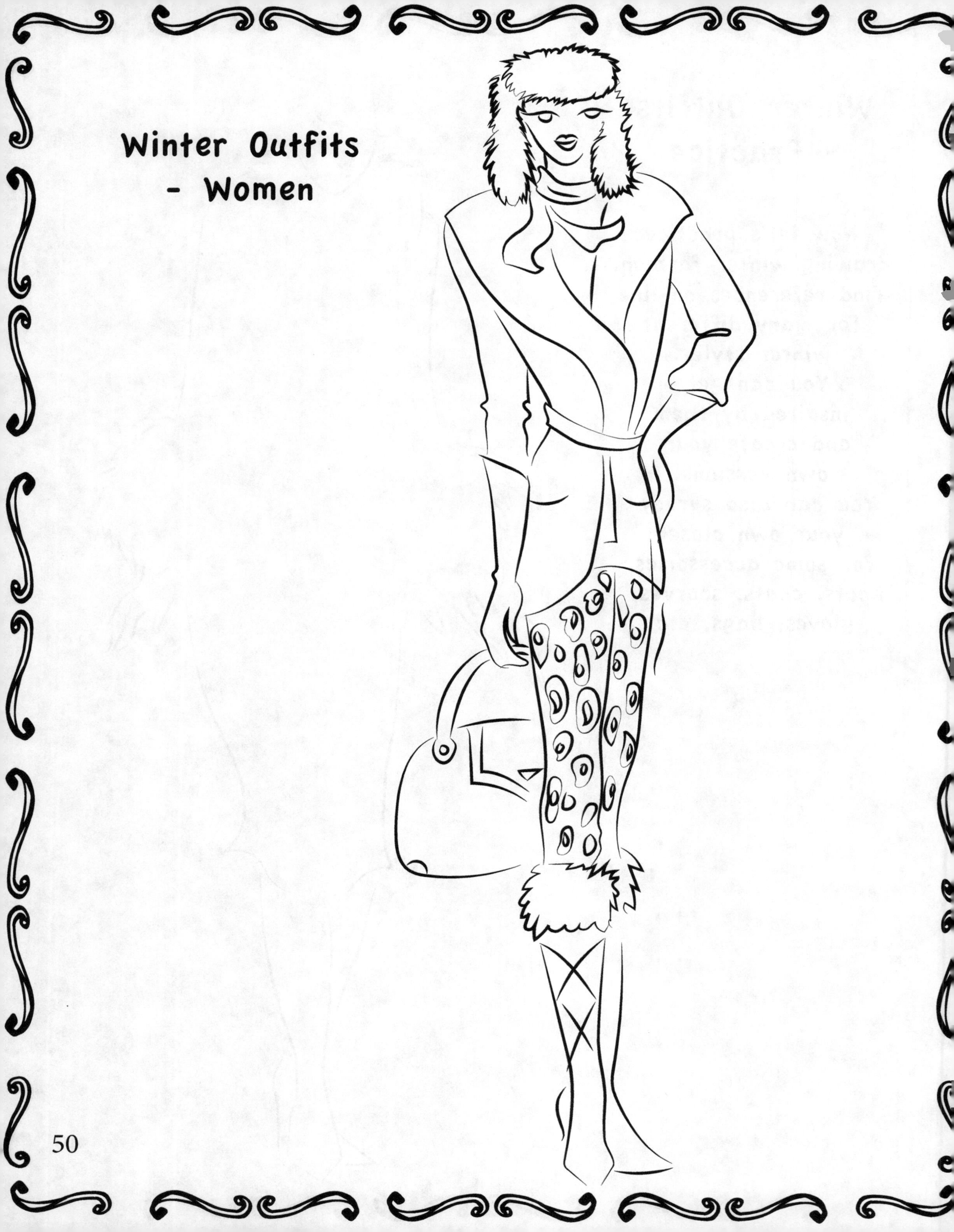
Winter Outfits
- Women

Winter Outfits - Practice

Now let's practice drawing winter fashion. Find references on-line for many different winter styles. You can get inspired by them and create your own versions. You can also survey your own closet for some accessories, boots, scarves, etc.

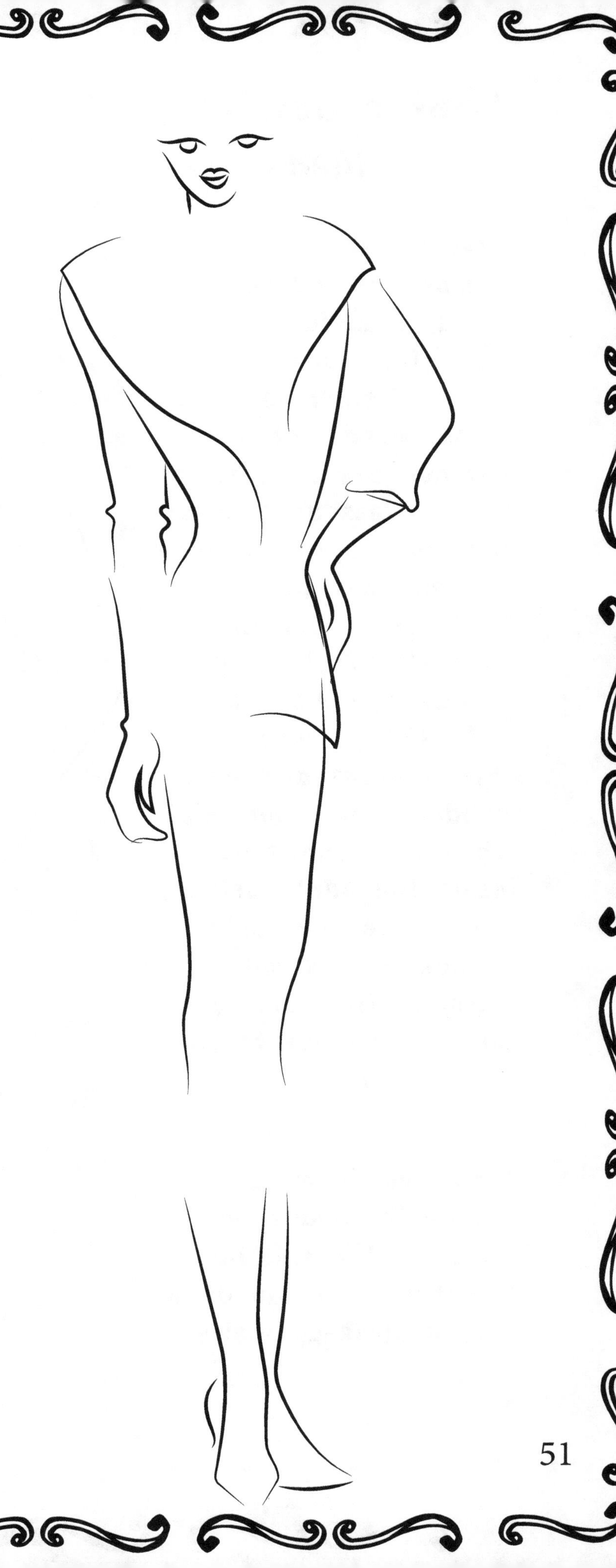

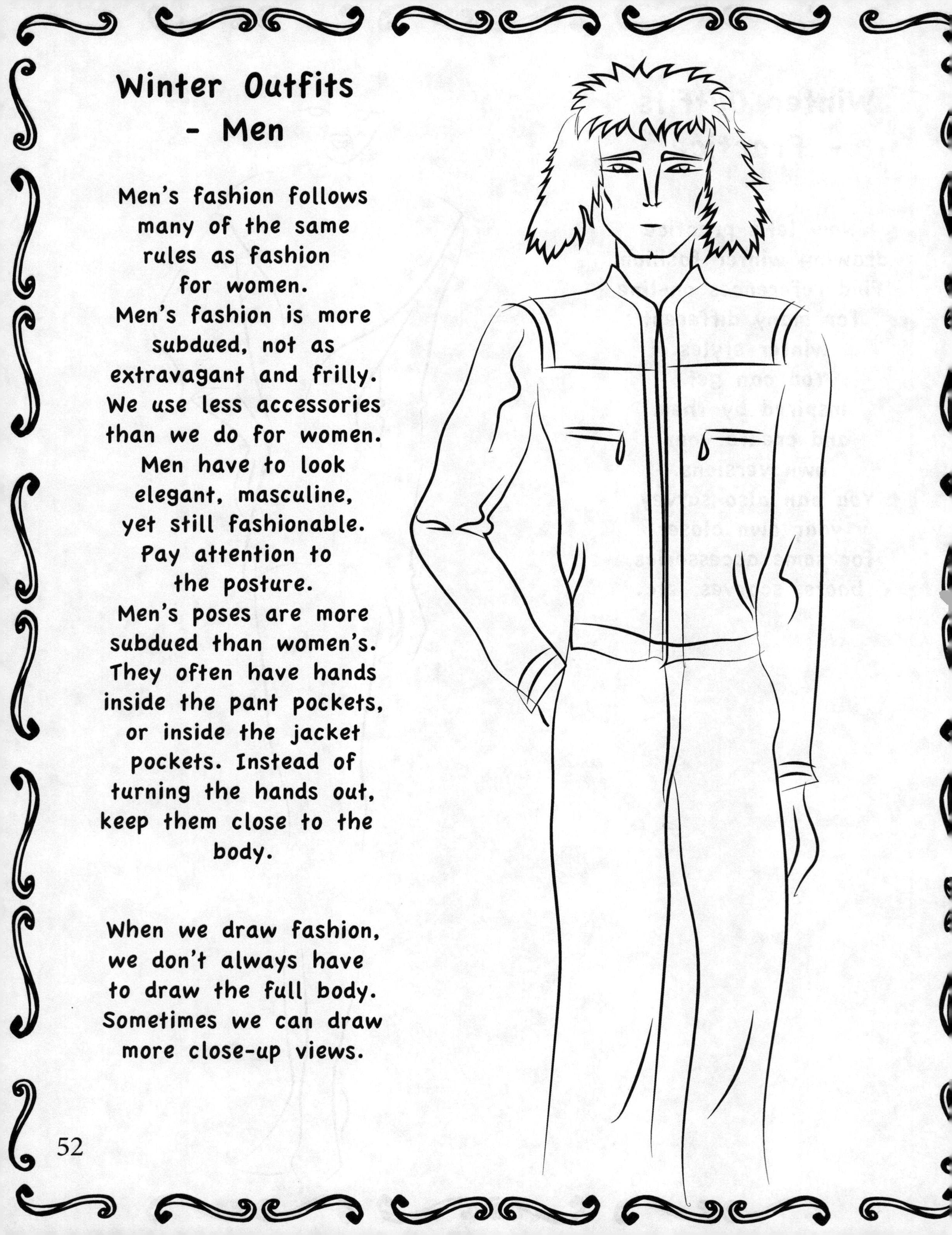

Winter Outfits - Men

Men's fashion follows many of the same rules as fashion for women.
Men's fashion is more subdued, not as extravagant and frilly.
We use less accessories than we do for women.
Men have to look elegant, masculine, yet still fashionable.
Pay attention to the posture.
Men's poses are more subdued than women's.
They often have hands inside the pant pockets, or inside the jacket pockets. Instead of turning the hands out, keep them close to the body.

When we draw fashion, we don't always have to draw the full body.
Sometimes we can draw more close-up views.

Winter Outfits - Men, Practice

Following the example on the left, draw the clothing on the male fashion figure.

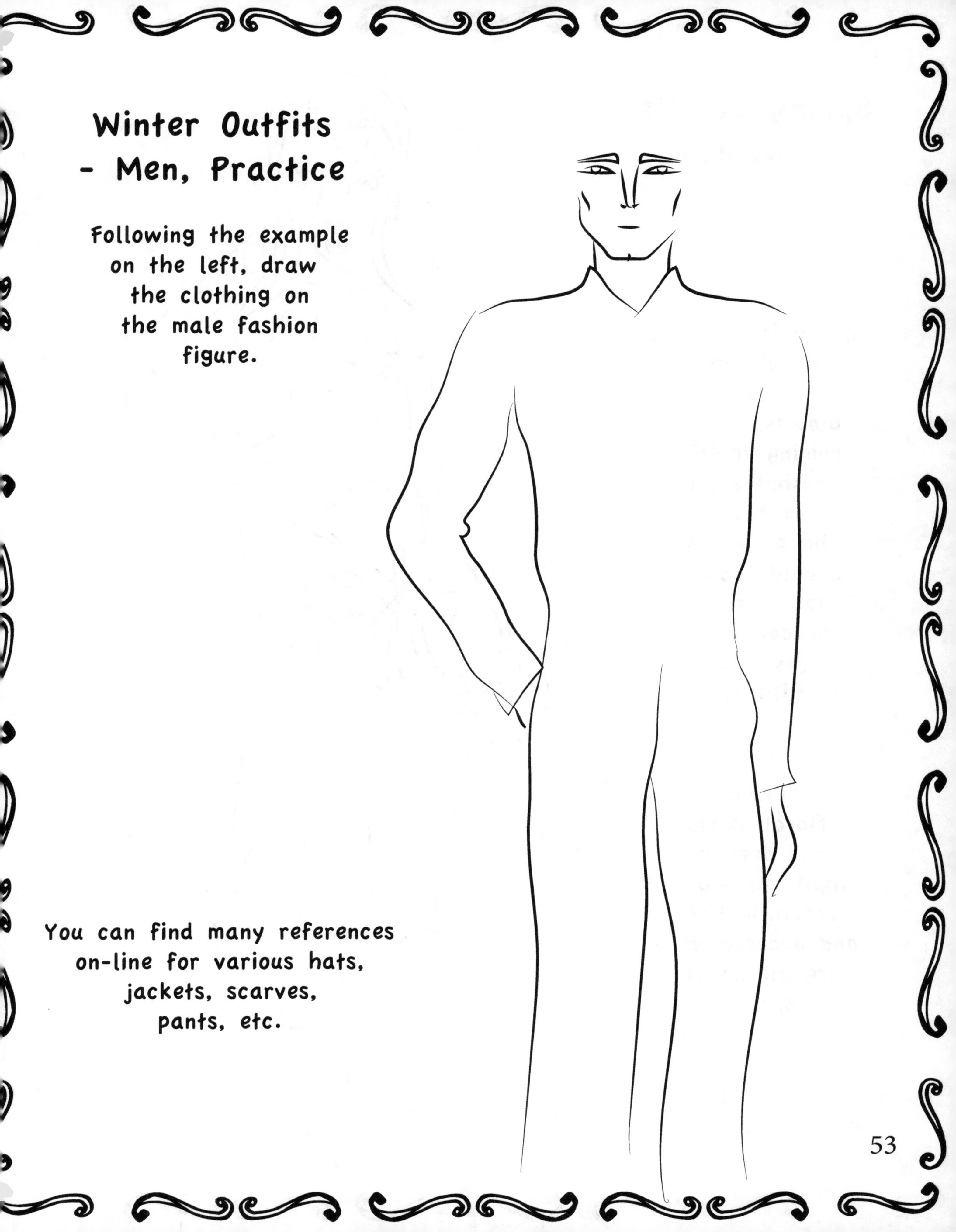

You can find many references on-line for various hats, jackets, scarves, pants, etc.

Spring Outfits - Women

Spring is the time of rebirth, rejuvenation, blooms, nature coming to life, freshness and lightness. The garments should show a lot of flow, gracefulness, joy and vitality.

Flowing floral skirts and dresses, light cardigans, romantic hats and accessories - are all about spring!

Spring Outfits
- Practice
Create your own
dresses and
prints!
Add hair and
accessories!
Have fun with
it and try
to portray
springtime
feeling in
the
outfits.

Spring Outfits
- Women

Spring Outfits
- Practice
Create your own
dresses and
prints!
Add hair and
accessories!
Have fun with
it and try
to portray
springtime
feeling in
the
outfits.

Spring Outfits - Men

Spring outfits for men tend to be more subdued than women's. A tee shirt and a light cardigan/ denim jacket plus jeans or slacks.

You can also accessorize with shades, belt, wristwatch, bag, scarf, etc.

Spring Outfits - Men Practice

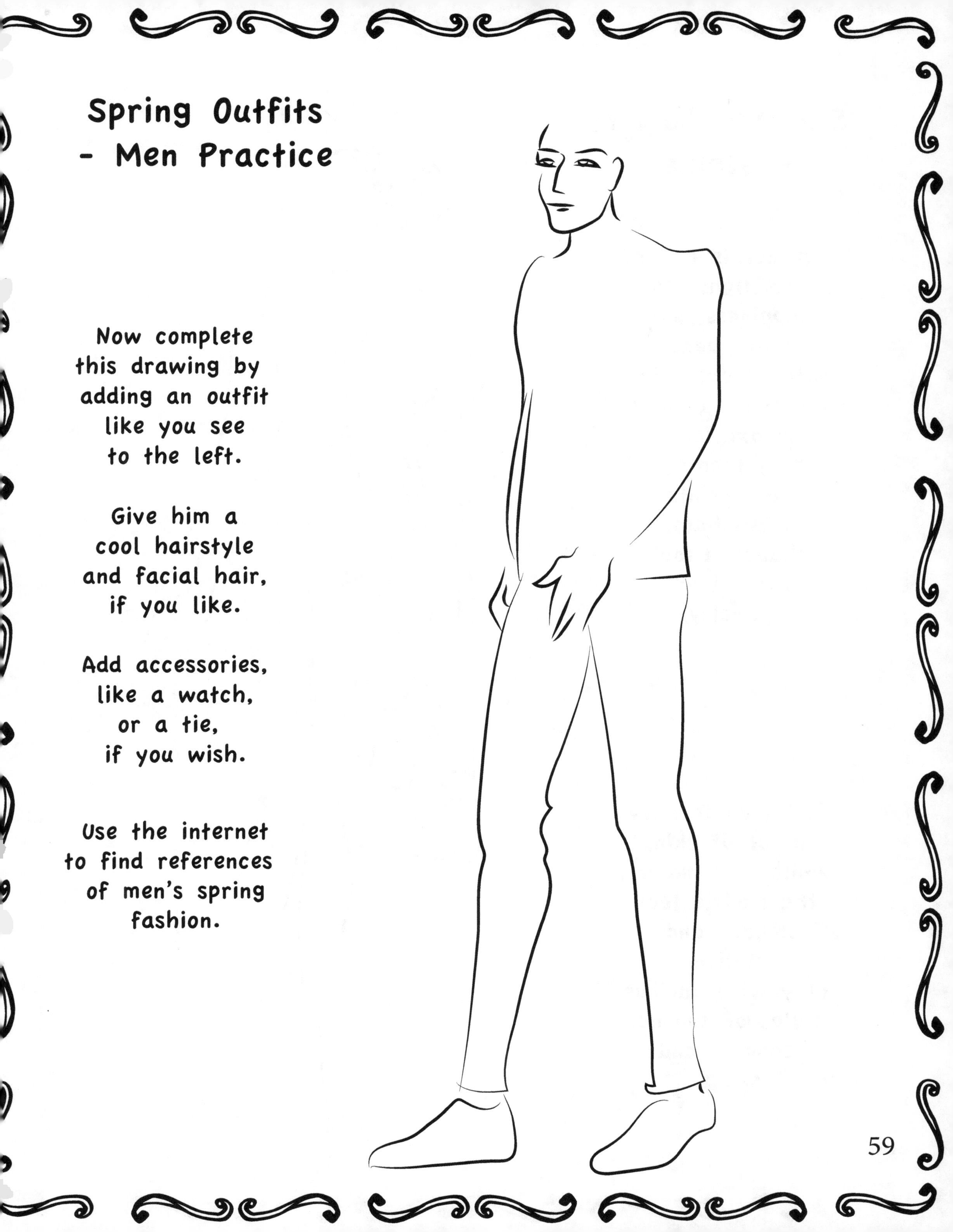

Now complete this drawing by adding an outfit like you see to the left.

Give him a cool hairstyle and facial hair, if you like.

Add accessories, like a watch, or a tie, if you wish.

Use the internet to find references of men's spring fashion.

Summer Outfits - Women

Summer is full of joy, lightness, happiness, sun, ocean, beach, outdoor activities, vacations, leisure relaxation, bright colors, bold prints, lavish hats, shades, beach bags, loud jewelry.

Feel free to show a lot of skin, while still making the models look elegant and stylish.
Play with various styles of summer sandals and shoes.

Summer Outfits
- Practice

Summer Outfits - Women

Summer is full of joy, lightness, happiness, sun, ocean, beach, outdoor activities, vacations, leisure relaxation, bright colors, bold prints, lavish hats, shades, beach bags, loud jewelry.

Feel free to show a lot of skin, while still making the models look elegant and stylish.
Play with various styles of summer sandals and shoes.

Summer Outfits - Practice

Now let's practice drawing summer fashion.
Find references on-line for many different summer styles.
You can get inspired by them and create your own versions.

You can also survey your own closet for some summer clothing, accessories, sunglasses, hats, shoes and jewelry.
You can come up with your own hair styles too.
You can add color after you are done, using light shading with color pencils, or gel pens.

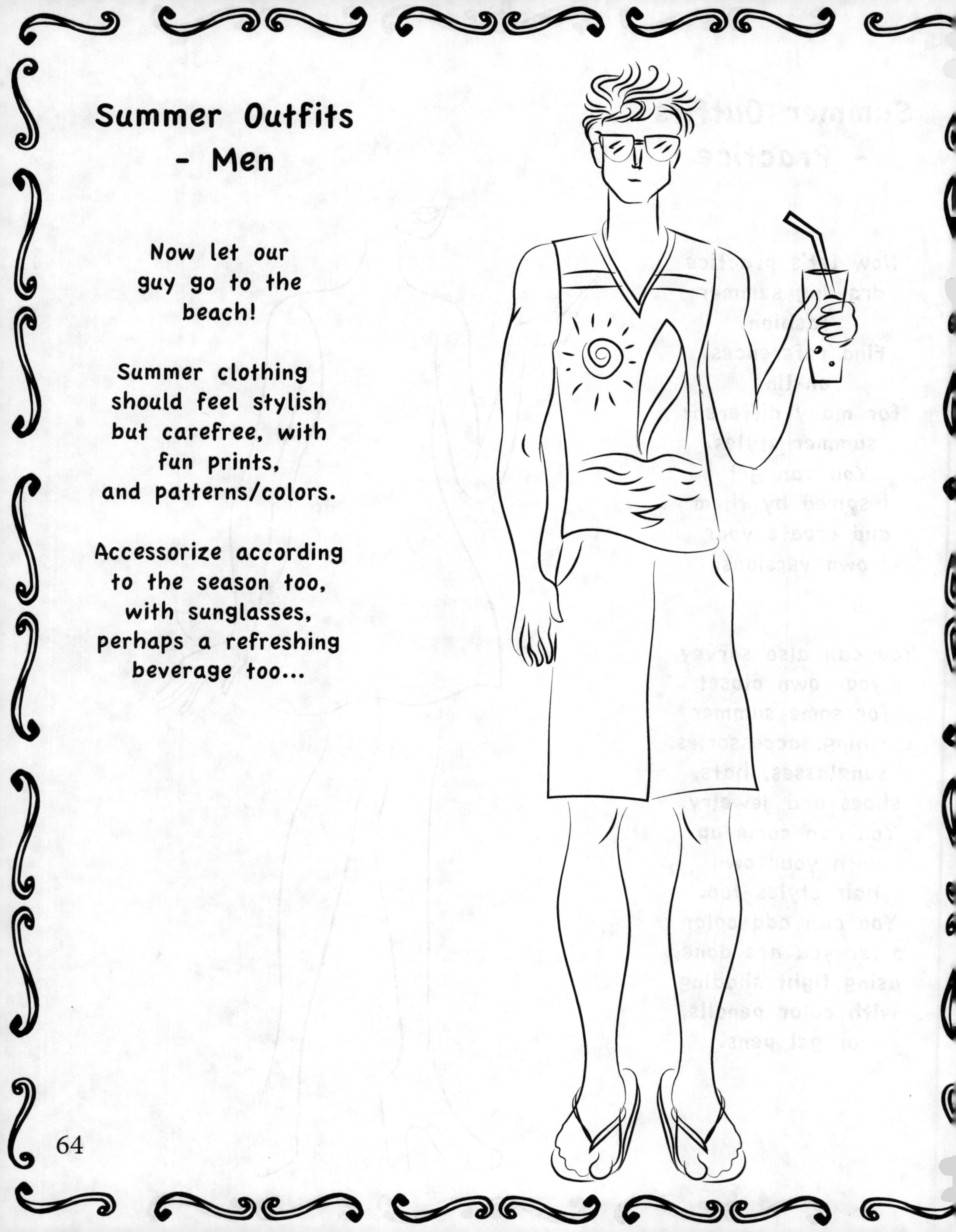

Summer Outfits - Men

Now let our guy go to the beach!

Summer clothing should feel stylish but carefree, with fun prints, and patterns/colors.

Accessorize according to the season too, with sunglasses, perhaps a refreshing beverage too...

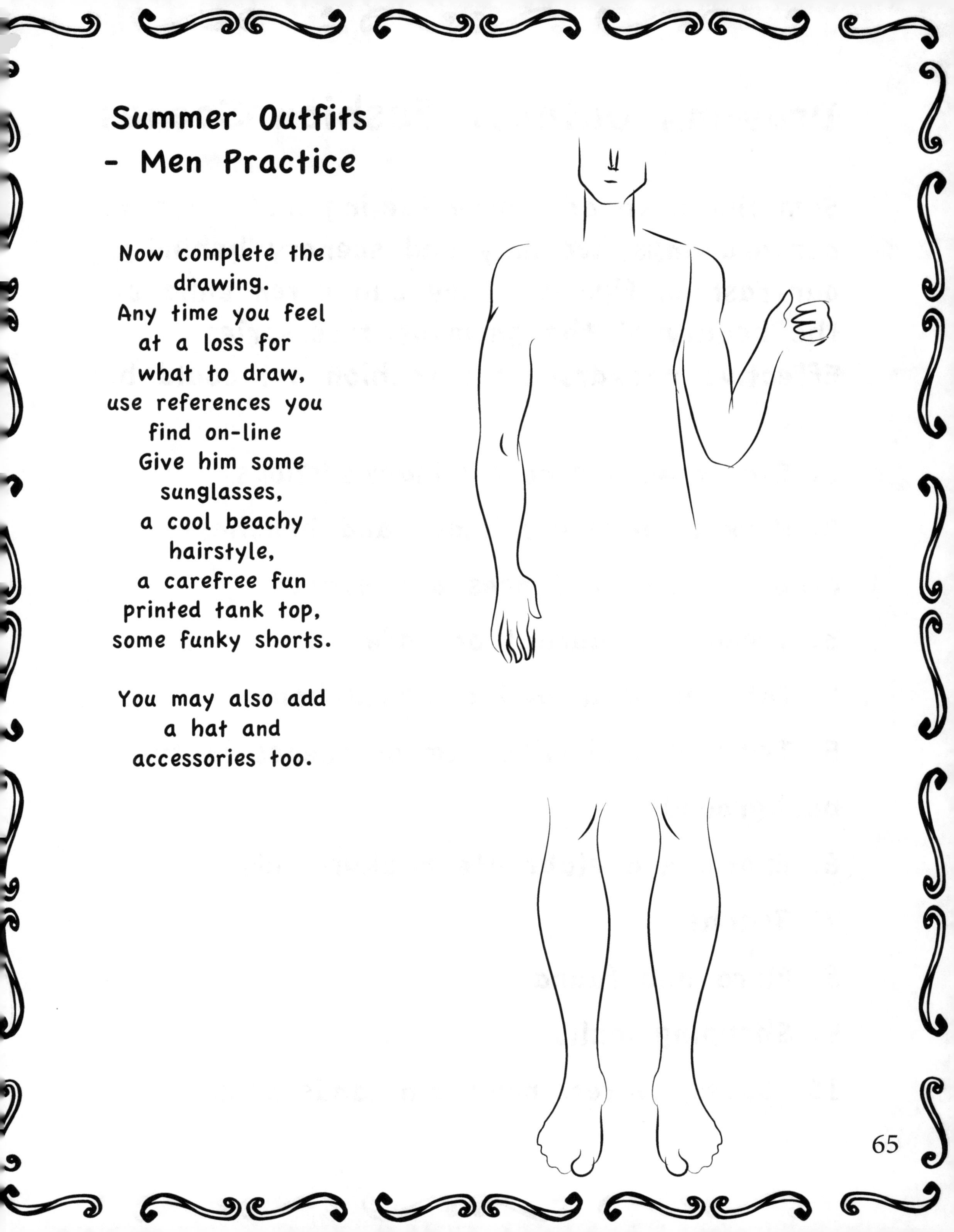

Summer Outfits - Men Practice

Now complete the drawing.
Any time you feel at a loss for what to draw, use references you find on-line
Give him some sunglasses, a cool beachy hairstyle, a carefree fun printed tank top, some funky shorts.

You may also add a hat and accessories too.

Drawing Outdoor Fashion Scenes

Sometimes, to add more feeling and mood to our drawings, we may add scenery behind our fashion figures. They can often enhance the beauty of the garment/accessories. Effective backdrops for fashion art could be:

1. Street with ornate windows/shops
2. Park with street lamps and benches/ ornate ironwork fences and arches
3. Trendy restaurant or cafe
4. Interior of a well designed home
5. Trips abroad with famous scenes in the background
6. Exotic and elaborate backgrounds
7. Beaches
8. Flora and fauna
9. Shopping malls
10. Boats, water, mountain landscapes

Drawing Outdoor Fashion Scenes

Street Scene and Practice

Look at the street scene to the left and try to draw it here.

Combine the street scene and the fashion figure. Tip: Draw the figure in the foreground before you draw the background.

Keep in mind that the figure has to be up-close and much bigger than the background, because it is in the foreground.

Try to combine the person and scene:

Drawing an Outdoor Paris Cafe

Now let's practice drawing it here:

Final Note

Now that we have gone over basic fashion drawing tips, it is time to practice our newly-acquired skills!

The best way to learn to draw well is to draw from life. You can grab some art pens, markers, pencils or watercolors and go to a park or beach. Look around for people who have interesting outfits. Draw them.

When you have a lot of practice drawing from life and/or reference, you will find that you can come up with interesting and creative outfits from your imagination. You can combine imagination and references for best results.

Most importantly, have fun! Don't feel that you have to make a perfect drawing, just draw every day, and you will become better and better!

Collect All of Our "How To Draw" and more books. Available at major retailers.

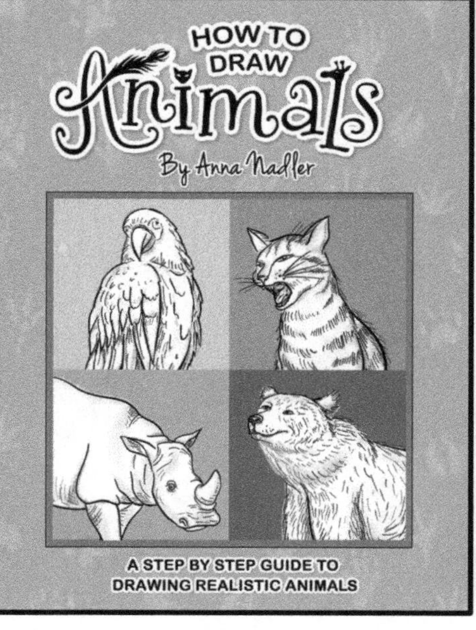

Printed in the USA
CPSIA information can be obtained
at www.ICGtesting.com
LVHW082309251123
764922LV00007B/630

9 781958 428177